Gardening Wit

summersdale

GARDENING WIT

Text contributed by Lucy York

Illustrations by Kath Walker

Summersdale Publishers Ltd
46 West Street
Chichester
West Sussex
PO19 1RP
UK

www.summersdale.com

Printed and bound in the UK by CPI Mackays, Chatham ME5 8TD

ISBN: 978-1-84024-786-2

Disclaimer
Every effort has been made to attribute the quotations in this collection to the correct source. Should there be any omissions or errors in this respect we apologise and shall be pleased to make the appropriate acknowledgements in any future edition.

Substantial discounts on bulk quantities of Summersdale books are available to corporations, professional associations and other organisations. For details telephone Summersdale Publishers on (+44-1243-771107), fax (+44-1243-786300) or email (nicky@summersdale.com).

Gardening Wit

Jane Brook

Contents

Editor's Note

The word 'anthology' comes from the Greek words *anthos*, flower, and *logia*, collection. Here, then, is a collection of flowerings of the imagination on all things garden-related, or, as Michel de Montaigne once put it, 'a posie of other men's flowers'.

Gardeners will know that whether you've got green fingers or you're all thumbs, gardening is hard work; there's seldom time to stop and smell the roses. In fact, Charles Dudley Warner may have been on to something when he said: 'What a man needs in gardening is a cast-iron back, with a hinge in it.'

Talking to oneself may be the first sign of madness, but talking to one's plants, it seems, may be the root of gardening success. So why not sling your hammock in the shade, and treat your precious perennials to an impromptu reading from this sumptuous harvest of cultivated cuttings and botanical banter for every season?

ALL THUMBS

I like to tease my plants. I water them with ice cubes.

Steven Wright

Never go to a doctor whose
office plants have died.

Erma Bombeck

———•———

I don't exactly have a green
thumb. I once killed a flagpole.

Milton Berle

———•———

Nothing grows in our
garden, only washing.

Dylan Thomas

A bachelor flat
is where all the
house plants are
dead but there's
something growing
in the refrigerator.

Marshall Williams

I consider every
plant hardy until I
have killed it myself.

Sir Peter Smithers

I have a rock garden. Last
week three of them died.

Richard Diran

❦

If you are not killing plants,
you are not really stretching
yourself as a gardener.

J. C. Raulston

❦

I don't have a green thumb. I
can't even get mould to grow
on last month's takeaway.

Johnny Gibson

Did you see the
pictures of the moon?
They must have the
same gardener I have.

Harry Hershfield

BLOOMING
MARVELLOUS

I used to wear a flower
in my lapel, but the
pot kept bumping
off my stomach.

Benny Hill

... I hold no preferences among
flowers, so long as they are
wild, free, spontaneous.
Bricks to all greenhouses!

Edward Abbey

——◆——

Any plant which, had it lived, would
have bloomed year after year.

Henry Beard defining a perennial

——◆——

What does the letter 'A' have
in common with a flower?
They both have bees
coming after them.

Kim Roblin

The time always turns
out to be 37 o'clock.

**Miles Kington on the exaggerated ability
of dandelions to tell the time**

❧

Magenta is the floral
form of original sin.

Gertrude Jekyll

❧

I'd like to buy a bunch of
flowers for the woman I love,
but my wife won't let me.

Henny Youngman

I want real flowers, perennials which
not only grow and change and die,
but also rise again and astonish me.

Emma L. Roth-Schwartz

When you have only two pennies
left in the world, buy a loaf of bread
with one and a lily with the other.

Chinese proverb

The Earth laughs in flowers.

Ralph Waldo Emerson

Children enjoy seeing
flowers coming up
– by the roots.

Erma Bombeck

Texture and foliage keep a
garden interesting through
the season. Flowers are just
moments of gratification.

Kevin Doyle

None can have a healthy love for
flowers unless he loves the wild ones.

Forbes Watson

Flowers are one of the few things
we buy and then watch die without
asking for our money back.

George Carlin

The actual flower is the plant's
highest fulfilment, and are not here
exclusively for herbaria, county
floras and plant geography: they
are here first of all for delight.

John Ruskin

❧

What a desolate place would
be a world without a flower! It
would be a face without a smile,
a feast without a welcome.

A. J. Balfour

❧

Flowers are love's truest language.

Park Benjamin

Almost every person, from
childhood, has been touched by the
untamed beauty of wildflowers.

Lady Bird Johnson, *Wildflowers Across America*

Each flower is a soul
opening out to nature.

Gérald de Nerva

GARDEN MANIA

An addiction to gardening is not all bad when you consider all the other choices in life.

Cora Lea Bell

Little by little, even with other cares, the slowly but surely working poison of the garden-mania begins to stir in my long-sluggish veins.

Henry James

My wife once described the garden as being ludicrous, which of course it is. But to me, ludicrous is good.

Bill Oddie

Never enough thyme in this garden of mine.

Anonymous

Let no one think that real gardening
is a bucolic and meditative
occupation. It is an insatiable
passion, like everything else to
which a man gives his heart.

Karel Capek

The love of gardening is a seed
once sown that never dies.

Gertrude Jekyll

No occupation is so delightful to me
as the culture of the earth, no culture
comparable to that of the garden.

Thomas Jefferson

There is more pleasure
in making a garden than in
contemplating a paradise.

Anne Scott-James

The trouble with
gardening is that it
does not remain an
avocation. It becomes
an obsession.

Phyllis McGinley

TROWEL AND ERROR

Everyone makes
mistakes, but no one
gets arrested for
killing their own plants.

Nigel Colborn

There are no gardening
mistakes, only experiments.

Janet Kilburn Phillips

A garden is always a series
of losses set against a few
triumphs, like life itself.

May Sarton

If garden beginners knew in
advance all the troubles in their
way, they might never begin.

Leonard H. Robbins

31

You must not know
too much or be too
precise or scientific
about birds and
trees and flowers and
watercraft; a certain
free-margin, and
even vagueness –
ignorance, credulity –
helps your enjoyment
of these things.

Henry David Thoreau

A garden is a thing of
beauty and a job forever.

Barry Tobin

Gardening is something you learn
by doing – and by making mistakes.

Carol Stocker

A WORM'S EYE VIEW

The smallest worm will turn, being trodden on.

William Shakespeare

The early bird gets the worm.
The early worm gets eaten.

Norman Augustine

We are all worms, but I do
believe that I am a glow worm.

Winston Churchill

Earthworms are the
intestines of the soil.

Aristotle

Our little kinsmen after rain
In plenty may be seen,
A pink and pulpy multitude
The tepid ground upon;
A needless life if seemed to me
Until a little bird
As to a hospitality
Advanced and breakfasted.

Emily Dickinson, *Our Little Kinsmen*

I think we consider too much the good luck of the early bird and not enough the bad luck of the early worm.

Franklin D. Roosevelt

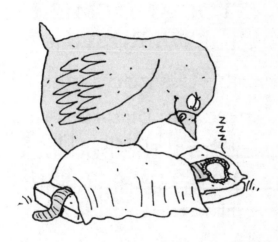

STOP AND SMELL
THE ROSES

I was flattered to
have a rose named
after me until I read
the description in the
catalogue: No good
in a bed, but perfect
up against a wall.

Eleanor Roosevelt

Where you tend a rose, my
lad, a thistle cannot grow.

Frances Hodgson Burnett

A rose by any other name
would be just as expensive.

Lambert Jeffries

I'd rather have roses on my table
than diamonds on my neck.

Emma Goldman

If seeds in the black earth can turn
into such beautiful roses, what might
not the heart of man become in its
long journey toward the stars?

G. K. Chesterton

The best rose-bush, after all, is not
that which has the fewest thorns, but
that which bears the finest roses.

Henry Van Dyke

It will never rain roses. When
we want to have more roses,
we must plant more roses.

George Eliot

A thorn defends the rose,
harming only those who
would steal the blossom.

Chinese proverb

I don't know whether nice people tend to grow roses or growing roses makes people nice.

Roland A. Browne

A rose is a rose is a rose.

Gertrude Stein

I haven't much time to be fond
of anything... But when I have a
moment's fondness to bestow,
most times... the roses get it.

William Wilkie Collins

God gave us our memories so that
we might have roses in December.

J. M. Barrie

We can complain
because rose bushes
have thorns, or
rejoice because thorn
bushes have roses.

Abraham Lincoln

TILL IT LIKE IT IS

To turn ordinary
clothes into gardening
clothes, simply mix
with compost.

Guy Browning

Gardening requires
lots of water – most
of it in the form of
perspiration.

Lou Erickson

If you think 'Hoe hoe' is a laughing matter, you're no gardener.

Herbert Prochnow

The longer I live the greater is my respect and affection for manure...

Elizabeth von Arnim

He who slings mud
generally loses ground.

Adlai E. Stevenson

Hoeing: a manual method of
severing roots from stems of newly
planted flowers and vegetables.

Henry Beard

You pray for rain, you gotta deal
with the mud too. That's a part of it.

Denzel Washington

After forking muck all day,
the apres-compost hot bath
is doubly rewarding.

Nigel Colborn

There is nothing pleasanter
than spading when the
ground is soft and damp.

John Steinbeck

Hoeing in the garden on a bright,
soft May day, when you are not
obligated to, is nearly equal to
the delight of going trouting.

Charles Dudley Warner

What this country needs is dirtier
fingernails and cleaner minds.

Will Rogers

To dig one's own spade into
one's own earth! Has life
anything better to offer...?

John Beverley Nichols

My wife's a water
sign. I'm an earth
sign. Together
we make mud.

Rodney Dangerfield

BUZZ OFF

Don't wear perfume
in the garden unless
you want to be
pollinated by bees.

Anne Raver

Bees are only dangerous if you
don't know what you're doing.

Michael Powell, *The Accidental Gardener*

The hum of bees is the
voice of the garden.

Elizabeth Lawrence

A bee is never as busy as it seems;
it's just that it can't buzz any slower.

Kin Hubbard

Why did the bees
go on strike?
For shorter flowers
and more honey.

Brian Johnston

Aerodynamically, the bumble
bee shouldn't be able to fly, but
the bumble bee doesn't know it
so it goes on flying anyway.

Mary Kay Ash

If a queen bee were crossed with
a Friesian bull, would not the
land flow with milk and honey?

Oliver St John

The pedigree of honey
Does not concern the bee;
A clover, any time, to him,
Is aristocracy.

Emily Dickinson

That which is not good for the
beehive cannot be good for the bees.

Marcus Aurelius

—••—

For cleanly and innocent bees, of
all other things, love and become,
and thrive in your orchard.

William Lawson, *A New Orchard and Garden*

The honey-bee's
great ambition is to be
rich, to lay up great
stores, to possess
the sweet of every
flower that blooms.

John Burroughs

COMMUNING
WITH NATURE

A garden is a friend
you can visit any time.

Anonymous

... a kind word every
now and then is
really quite enough.

Victoria Glendinning on talking to flowers

When I talk to plants
they respond to me.

Prince Charles

As I work among my flowers, I find
myself talking to them, reasoning
and remonstrating with them, and
adoring them as if they were human
beings. Much laughter I provoke
among my friends by so doing, but
that is of no consequence. We are
on such good terms, my flowers and I.

Celia Thaxter, *An Island Garden*

Shall I not have intelligence with
the earth? Am I not partly leaves
and vegetable mould myself?

Henry David Thoreau

The good plant has to be
able to live amicably with
other plants in the border.

Richardson Wright

Plants are like people: they're all
different and a little bit strange.

John Kehoe

PEST BEHAVIOUR

The ant is knowing
and wise, but he
doesn't know enough
to take a vacation.

Clarence Day

If I outrun 'em round the yard, how come they beat me to the chard?

Allen Klein on snails

We have descended into the garden and caught three hundred slugs. How I love the mixture of the beautiful and the squalid in gardening. It makes it so lifelike.

Evelyn Underhill

I bought an ant farm. I don't know where I am going to get a tractor that small!

Steven Wright

It seems to me the worst of all the plagues is the slug, the snail without a shell. He is beyond description repulsive, a mass of sooty, shapeless slime, and he devours everything.

Celia Thaxter, *An Island Garden*

The problem with picnics is
that they're always held on a
holiday – when the ants
have the day off too.

Gene Perret

Did you know that ducks are
natural predators of slugs? As
the old saying goes, if you have
too many slugs the chances are
you have a deficiency of ducks.

Michael Powell, *The Accidental Gardener*

Do what we can, summer
will have its flies.

Ralph Waldo Emerson

I cannot believe the objection
oftenest made to me: that
mosquitoes prevent the enjoyment
of a garden. True as it is in
part, it is true only for certain
seasons and for certain hours of
the day. Mosquitoes never yet
kept anyone who really wanted
a garden from having one.

H. G. Dwight, 'Gardens and
Gardens', *Atlantic Monthly*

What would become of the garden
if the gardener treated all the
weeds and slugs and birds and
trespassers as he would like to be
treated, if he were in their place?

Thomas Henry Huxley

CULTIVATE YOUR
MIND, BODY AND SOUL

Gardening is the
purest of human
pleasures.

Sir Francis Bacon

Regular bouts of gentle weeding,
digging and mowing can revitalise
a man's flagging sex drive.

David Derbyshire in the *Daily Mail*

Gardening and laughing are
two of the best things in life you
can do to promote good health
and a sense of well being.

David Hobson

Gardening is the only
unquestionably useful job.

George Bernard Shaw

75

The garden is
a ground plot
for the mind.

Thomas Hill

We may think we're nurturing
our garden but of course it's our
garden that is really nurturing us.

Jenny Uglow

———•———

A garden is a grand teacher. It
teaches patience and careful
watchfulness; it teaches industry and
thrift; above all it teaches entire trust.

Gertrude Jekyll

———•———

Study nature, love nature, stay
close to nature. It will never fail you.

Frank Lloyd Wright

A modest garden contains, for those
who know how to look and to wait,
more instruction than a library.

Henri Frédéric Amiel

My garden of flowers is also
my garden of thoughts and
dreams. The thoughts grow
as freely as the flowers, and
the dreams are as beautiful.

Abram L. Urban

Who has learned to garden
who did not at the same time
learn to be patient?

H. L. V. Fletcher

As long as one has a garden,
one has a future. As long as
one has a future, one is alive.

Frances Hodgson Burnett, *The Secret Garden*

He who cultivates a garden, and
brings to perfection flowers and
fruits cultivates and advances at
the same time his own nature.

Ezra Weston

THE GARDEN OF EVE

You can lead a
horticulture but you
can't make her think.

Dorothy Parker

An Englishman's home may be
his castle, but it's the grounds that
the Englishwoman cares about.

Wendy Holden

I get a lot of flak from people who
say you can't be a real gardener
and try to grow your nails. But I
wear gloves for serious gardening.

Rachel de Thame

I always think of my sins when I weed.
They grow apace in the same way
and are harder still to get rid of.

Helena Rutherfurd Ely, *A Woman's Hardy Garden*

It has been said that vines are to
bits of architecture what a dress is
to a woman. It may serve to enhance
beauty or to cover defects.

Loring Underwood

The husbands may mow the
lawn, but it's the women who do
the planting, the digging, the
weeding and all the real work that
goes into making a garden.

Charlie Dimmock

A man should never
plant a garden
larger than his wife
can take care of.

T. H. Everett

THE ROOT TO SUCCESS

As is the garden
such is the gardener.
A man's nature
runs either to
herbs or weeds.

Francis Bacon

Green fingers are made, not born;
success comes to all, with practice.

Nigel Colborn

A gardener is a bloke
who calls a spade a spade
– until he falls over one.

George Coote

...they are always optimistic, always
enterprising, and never satisfied.

Vita Sackville-West on gardeners

I have nothing against gardening. I just prefer not to be there when it happens.

Tracy McLeod

I'm not a dirt gardener. I sit with my walking stick and point things out that need to be done. After many years the garden is now totally obedient.

Sir Edwin Hardy Amies

I want easy-care plants with extended interest.

Judy Glattstein

Among gardeners, enthusiasm
and experience rarely exist
in equal measures.

Roger B. Swain

Green fingers are the extension
of a verdant heart.

Russell Page

Gardeners, I think, dream bigger
dreams than emperors.

Mary Cantwell

Whoever said that
to be happy for an
hour you should get
drunk but to be happy
for a lifetime, plant
a garden, missed an
obvious opportunity:
to get drunk *and*
plant a garden.

Michael Powell, *The Accidental Gardener*

BEE INSPIRED

In his garden every
man may be his own
artist without apology
or explanation.

Louise Beebe Wilder

I have never had so many
good ideas day after day as
when I work in the garden.

John Erskine

I perhaps owe having become
a painter to flowers.

Claude Monet

Art is the unceasing effort to
compete with the beauty of
flowers and never succeeding.

Marc Chagall

Should it not be remembered
that in setting a garden we
are painting a picture?

Beatrix Jones Farrand

Half the interest of a garden
is the constant exercise of the
imagination. I believe that people
entirely devoid of imagination never
can be really good gardeners.

Mrs C. W. Earle

We might as well abandon
our spades and pitchforks
as pretend that nature is
everything and art nothing.

James Shirley Hibberd

Gardening is the art that uses
flowers and plants as paint, and
the soil and sky as canvas.

Elizabeth Murray

Plant trees – they give us two
of the most crucial elements for
survival: oxygen and books.

Whitney Brown

There is a myth that if you
write about gardens you must
have a perfect garden.

Kate Copsey

———◆———

I would rather do a good hours
work weeding than write two
pages of my best; nothing is so
interesting as weeding. I went
crazy over the outdoor work,
and at last had to confine myself
to the house, or literature must
have gone by the board.

Robert Louis Stevenson

I am writing in the garden. To write as one should of a garden one must write not outside it or merely somewhere near it, but in the garden.

Frances Hodgson Burnett

PEAS AND
TRANQUILLITY

A garden is the best
alternative therapy.

Germaine Greer

I think that if ever a mortal heard
the voice of God it would be in a
garden at the cool of the day.

F. Frankfort Moore

Flowers have a mysterious and
subtle influence upon the feelings,
not unlike some strains of music.
They relax the tenseness of the
mind. They dissolve its vigour.

Henry Ward Beecher

There is peace in the garden.
Peace and results.

Ruth Stout

For me, a garden is peace of mind...

Henry Louis Gates Jr

How fair is a garden amid the
trials and passions of existence.

Benjamin Disraeli

Gardening is a labour full of
tranquillity and satisfaction;
natural and instructive, and
as such contributes to the
most serious contemplation,
experience, health and longevity.

John Evelyn

101

I used to visit and revisit it a dozen times a day, and stand in deep contemplation over my vegetable progeny with a love that nobody could share or conceive of who had never taken part in the process of creation.

Nathaniel Hawthorne, *Mosses from an Old Manse*

GROUND RULES

One of the worst
mistakes you can make
as a gardener is to
think you're in charge.

Janet Gillespie

Heed the experts, but don't
take them too seriously.

Nigel Colborn

The best fertiliser is the
gardener's shadow.

Anonymous

The golden rule of gardening
is to pay attention to local
conditions of weather and soil.

Carol Williams

If a person cannot love a plant
after he has pruned it, then
he has either done a poor job
or is devoid of emotion.

Liberty Hyde Bailey

Other people's tools work only
in other people's gardens.

Arthur Bloch, *Murphy's Law and Other
Reasons Why Things Go Wrong*

...the constitution of Paul
Bunyan and the basic
training of a commando.

S. J. Perelman on the characteristics
required for gardening

It is a golden maxim to
cultivate the garden
for the nose, and
the eyes will take
care of themselves.

Robert Louis Stevenson

SWEET CONTENTMENT

To be overcome
by the fragrance of
flowers is a delectable
form of defeat.

Beverley Nichols

Flowers never emit so sweet and
strong a fragrance as before a storm.

Jean Paul Richter

—◆—

Perfumes are the feelings of flowers.

Heinrich Heine

—◆—

With a few flowers in my garden,
half a dozen pictures and some
books, I live without envy.

Lope de Vega

I do not think I have ever seen anything more beautiful than the bluebell I have been looking at.

Gerard Manley Hopkins

The flower is the poetry of reproduction. It is an example of the eternal seductiveness of life.

Jean Giraudoux

Flowers always make people better, happier, and more helpful; they are sunshine, food and medicine for the soul.

Luther Burbank

Where flowers bloom so does hope.

Lady Bird Johnson, *Public Roads: Where Flowers Bloom*

People from a planet without flowers would think we must be mad with joy the whole time to have such things about us.

Iris Murdoch

How could such sweet and wholesome hours be reckoned, but in herbs and flowers?

Andrew Marvell

Who would have
thought it possible
that a tiny little flower
could preoccupy a
person so completely
that there simply
wasn't room for any
other thought...

Sophie Scholl

What a pity flowers can utter
no sound! – A singing rose, a
whispering violet, a murmuring
honeysuckle... oh, what a rare and
exquisite miracle would these be!

Henry Ward Beecher

To analyse the charms of
flowers is like dissecting music;
it is one of those things which
it is far better to enjoy, than to
attempt to fully understand.

Henry T. Tuckerman

LABOUR AND WAIT

An optimistic
gardener is one
who believes that
whatever goes down
must come up.

Lesley Hall

... with a spade and a package
of garden seeds.

Dan Bennett on how to gamble healthily

❦

When gardeners garden, it is
not just plants that grow, but
the gardeners themselves.

Ken Druse

❦

Plant orders do not arrive on
sunny, warm Saturday mornings.

Steve Hatch

Gardening is the slowest
of the performing arts.

Mac Griswold

———•———

Every man reaps what he sows in this
life – except the amateur gardener.

Lesley Hall

———•———

One of the most delightful
things about a garden is the
anticipation it provides.

W. E. Johns

THE GARDEN OF EATIN'

It's obvious that
carrots are good for
your eyesight. Have
you ever seen a rabbit
wearing glasses?

Steve McQueen

You can spray them with acid,
beat them with sticks and
burn them; they love it.

S. J. Perelman on the hardiness of tomatoes

❦

There's no getting blood
out of a turnip.

Frederick Marryat

❦

... interesting but lack a sense of
purpose when unaccompanied
by a good cut of meat.

Fran Lebowitz on vegetables

For all things produced in a garden,
whether of salads or fruits, a poor
man will eat better that has one of his
own, than a rich man that has none.

John Claudius Loudon

Most plants taste better when
they've had to suffer a little.

Diana Kennedy

He who sows peas on the
highway does not get all
the pods into his barn.

Danish proverb

Cabbage: a vegetable about as large and wise as a man's head.

Ambrose Bierce, *The Devil's Dictionary*

I do not like broccoli. And I haven't liked it since I was a little kid and my mother made me eat it. And I'm President of the United States and I'm not going to eat any more broccoli.

George Bush

What did the carrot
say to the wheat?
Lettuce rest, I'm feeling beet.

Shel Silverstein

Can the garden afford any
thing more delightful to view
than those forests of asparagus,
artichokes, lettuce, peas, beans
and other legumes and edulous
plants so different in colour
and of such various shapes...

Stephen Switzer, *The Practical Gardener*

As for vegetables, I do not
consider a plot of ground devoted
to them worthy of the honourable
name of garden. Vegetables are,
of course, a part of gardening,
but the least, the last, for those
who do not have to raise them,
the most dishonourable part.

H. G. Dwight, 'Gardens and
Gardening', *Atlantic Monthly*

Life expectancy would grow by leaps
and bounds if green vegetables
smelled as good as bacon.

Doug Larson

There is nothing that is comparable to it, as satisfactory or as thrilling, as gathering the vegetables one has grown.

Alice B. Toklas

What was paradise, but a garden full of vegetables and herbs and pleasure? Nothing there but delights.

William Lawson

Lettuce is like conversation:
it must be fresh and crisp, and
so sparkling that you scarcely
notice the bitter in it.

Charles Dudley Warner

He had been eight years upon a
project for extracting sunbeams
out of cucumbers, which were
to be put into vials hermetically
sealed, and let out to warm the
air in raw, inclement summers.

Jonathan Swift, *Gulliver's Travels*

I was a vegetarian until I started
leaning towards sunlight.

Rita Rudner

... the rows of cabbages are a series
of little silver waterfalls in the moon.

Carl Sandburg on a garden in the moonlight

Let first the onion flourish there,
Rose among the roots,
the maiden-fair
Wine scented and poetic soul
of the capacious salad bowl.

Robert Louis Stevenson

It's difficult to think anything
but pleasant thoughts while
eating a home-grown tomato.

Lewis Grizzard

Sex is good, but not as good
as fresh, sweet corn.

Garrison Keillor

A cauliflower is
a cabbage with a
college education.

Mark Twain

WHERE THE GRASS IS GREENER

If the grass is greener in the other fellow's garden, let him worry about mowing it.

Paddy Murray

The kind of grass I've got in
the garden lies down under
the mower and pops up again
as soon as it's passed.

Basil Boothroyd

A perfect summer day is when
the sun is shining, the breeze is
blowing, the birds are singing,
and the lawn mower is broken.

James Dent

Grass is the cheapest plant to install
and the most expensive to maintain.

Pat Howell

I always thought a yard was three
feet, then I started mowing the lawn.

C. E. Cowman

There is not a sprig of grass that
shoots uninteresting to me.

Thomas Jefferson

If dandelions were hard to grow, they
would be most welcome on any lawn.

Andrew V. Mason

The grass is always greener
over the septic tank.

Erma Bombeck

Fences have nothing to do
with it. The grass is greenest
where it is watered.

Robert Fulghum

A lawn is nature under
totalitarian rule.

Michael Pollan

Nothing is more pleasant to the eye
than green grass kept finely shorn.

Francis Bacon

Grass is hard and
lumpy and damp,
and full of dreadful
black insects.

Oscar Wilde

WATER YOU
WAITING FOR?

The watering of a
garden requires as
much judgement as the
seasoning of a soup.

Helena Rutherford Ely

The frog does not drink up
the pond in which he lives.

American Indian saying

—◦—

Advice to those about to build a
water garden – DON'T. Not that
the water garden is not a joy and
a glory; but that it is cruelly hard
to keep in order and control.

R. J. Farrer, *Alpines and Bog Plants*

—◦—

For fountains, they are a Great
Beauty and Refreshment, but
Pools mar all, and make the
Garden unwholesome, and
full of Flies and Frogs.

Sir Francis Bacon, *Of Gardens*

137

To a gardener
there is nothing
more exasperating
than a hose that just
isn't long enough.
Cecil Roberts

A pool is the eye of the garden
in whose candid depths is
mirrored its advancing grace.

Louise Bebe Wilder

Remember to turn the golden
orfe twice a week, as the same
view can get very boring for
large fish in a small pond.

Michael Powell, *The Accidental Gardener*

ALL CREATURES
GREAT AND SMALL

Life is hard for
insects. And don't
think mice are having
any fun either.

Woody Allen

When you have seen one
ant, one bird, one tree, you
have not seen them all.

E. O. Wilson

Toads may not be the prettiest
creatures, but they are a great
help in the garden as they
love to munch on slugs.

Isobel Carlson, *A Miscellany of Garden Wisdom*

A cow is a very good animal in the field; but we turn her out of a garden.

Samuel Johnson

The spider's touch, how
exquisitely fine!
Feels at each thread, and
lives along the line.

Alexander Pope

The fox has many tricks.
The hedgehog has but one.
But that is the best of all.

Desiderius Erasmus

If you want to live and thrive,
let the spider run alive.

American Quaker saying

The toad has indeed no superior
as a destroyer of noxious insects,
and he possesses no bad habits
and is entirely inoffensive himself,
every owner of a garden should
treat him with utmost hospitality.

Celia Thaxter, *An Island Garden*

A prudent man does not make
the goat his gardener.

Hungarian proverb

I do believe that an intimacy
with the world of crickets and
their kind can be salutary.

Howard E. Evans

———❦———

Deep in the sun-searched
growths the dragonfly
Hangs like a blue thread
loosened from the sky.

Dante Gabriel Rossetti

———❦———

A garden without cats, it will be
generally agreed, can scarcely
deserve to be called a garden at all.

Beverly Nichols

146

Toads are
conservative animals,
I think, and not much
given to expecting the
best from fortune.

Henry Mitchell

HERE'S LOOKIN'
AT YEW

A garden without
trees scarcely
deserves to be
called a garden.

Henry Ellacombe

Trees display the effects
of breeding quite as much
as horses, dogs or men.

William Howitt

———◆———

There are those who say that
trees shade the garden too much,
and interfere with the growth
of the vegetables. There may
be something in this: but when
I go down the potato rows, the
rays of the sun glancing upon
my shining blade, the sweat
pouring down my face, I should
be grateful for shade.

Charles Dudley Warner

I never saw a discontented tree.
They grip the ground as though
they liked it, and though fast rooted
they travel about as far as we do.

John Muir

Solitary trees, if they grow
at all, grow strong.

Winston Churchill

A tree growing out of the ground
is as wonderful today as it ever
was. It does not need to adopt
new and startling methods.

Robert Henri

Every tree has its own place upon this earth. Only man has lost his way.

Margaret Craven

Great trees are good for nothing but shade.

George Herbert

For sale: bonsai tree. Large.

Jimmy Carr

Trees are much like
human beings and
enjoy each other's
company. Only a few
love to be alone.

Jens Jensen

The true meaning of life is to
plant trees, under whose shade
you do not expect to sit.

Nelson Henderson

———•———

He who plants a tree plants a hope.

Lucy Larcom

———•———

... they seem more resigned
to the way they have to live
than other things do.

Willa Cather on the qualities of trees

Except during the nine months
before he draws his first breath,
no man manages his affairs
as well as a tree does.

George Bernard Shaw

The wonder is that we can see
these trees and not wonder more.

Ralph Waldo Emerson

You can't be suspicious of
a tree, or accuse a bird or a
squirrel of subversion.

Hal Borland

155

FRUITS OF LABOUR

In an orchard there
should be enough
to eat, enough to
lay up, enough to be
stolen, and enough to
rot on the ground.

James Boswell

I think that if you shake the tree,
you ought to be around when
the fruit falls to pick it up.

Mary Cassatt

'Would you like some manure for
your rhubarb?' 'No, we always
have ice cream on ours.'

Brendan Grace

Strawberries are the angels of the
earth, innocent and sweet with green
leafy wings reaching heavenward.

Jasmine Heiler

Even if I knew that tomorrow
the world would go to pieces, I
would still plant my apple tree.

Martin Luther

And the fruits will outdo what
the flowers have promised.

Francois de Malherbe

A man is old when he can
pass an apple orchard and not
remember the stomach ache.

James Russell Lowell

Avoid suspicion: when you're
walking through your neighbour's
melon patch, don't tie your shoe.

Chinese proverb

If you treat your plants like members
of your family, they will thrive. But
you mustn't get sentimental when it's
time to stuff them in the wheelie bin.

Michael Powell, *The Accidental Gardener*

GNOME MAN'S LAND

... diddy men have cropped up in European gardens, on doorsteps, not doing much, tripping people over.

Zoe Williams on gnomes over the years

I was turned down as a bus
conductor for being too tall,
and I couldn't see myself making
garden gnomes with my brother
for the rest of my days.

John Major on why he decided to go into politics

People enjoy gnomes. They make
them smile and they will be here
for many generations to come.

Margaret Egleton, founder of the Gnomeland website

To a lot of people they're probably
just garden ornaments. But
to me they're part of the family.

Bill Gilbertson from Bolton, who woke up
one morning to find his entire collection of
over forty gnomes had been stolen

When you read these few words, we will no longer be part of your selfish world, where we serve merely as decoration.

'Suicide' note left by the Garden Gnome Liberation Front next to eleven gnomes that had been kidnapped from various gardens in France and were left hanging from a bridge

A GARDEN FOR ALL SEASONS (AND ALL WEATHERS)

The gardening season officially begins on January 1st and ends on December 31st.

Marie Huston

There ought to be gardens for
all months in the year, in which,
severally, things of beauty
may be then in season.

Sir Francis Bacon

Climate is what we expect,
weather is what we get.

Mark Twain

God made rainy days so gardeners
could get the housework done.

Anonymous

All through the long winter, I dream
of my garden. On the first day
of spring, I dig my fingers deep
into the soft earth. I can feel its
energy, and my spirits soar.

Helen Hayes

It's Mother Nature's way of telling
me flowers get more sex than I do.

Basil White on why he dislikes allergy season

I love spring anywhere, but
if I could choose I would
always greet it in a garden.

Ruth Stout

Spring unlocks the flowers
to paint the laughing soil.

Reginald Heber

Spring has come when you put
your foot on three daisies.

Barbara Barger

April comes like an idiot,
babbling and strewing flowers.

Edna St Vincent Millay

In the spring, at the end of the
day, you should smell like dirt.

Margaret Atwood

Summer has set in with
its usual severity.

Samuel Taylor Coleridge

Deep summer is when laziness
finds respectability.

Sam Keen

April showers bring May flowers.

Proverb

... there is a harmony
In autumn, and a lustre in its sky,
Which through the summer
is not heard or seen,
As if it could not be, as
if it had not been!

Percy Bysshe Shelley, *Hymn to Intellectual Beauty*

Bulb: potential flower buried in
Autumn, never to be seen again.

Henry Beard

... brown, red and yellow – just like
the decayed food in my fridge.

Bob Monkhouse on the colours of autumn

Leaves are verbs that
conjugate the seasons.

Gretel Ehrlich

I cannot endure to waste anything
as precious as autumn sunshine
by staying in the house. So I
spend almost all the daylight
hours in the open air.

Nathaniel Hawthorne

Delicious autumn! My very soul
is wedded to it, and if I were a
bird I would fly about the earth
seeking the successive autumns.

George Eliot

There's one good thing about
snow – it makes your lawn look
as nice as your neighbour's.

Clyde Moore

If we had no winter, the spring
would not be so pleasant.

Anne Bradstreet

Autumn is a second spring
when every leaf is a flower.

Albert Camus

GOING CHEEP

When birds burp, it must taste like bugs.

Bill Watterson

Rise early. It is the early bird that
catches the worm. Don't be fooled
by this absurd saw; I once knew
a man who tried it. He got up at
sunrise and a horse bit him.

Mark Twain

———

Birds are messy eaters so
locate bird tables in a spot that
does not need to be pristine.

Isobel Carlson, *A Miscellany of Garden Wisdom*

———

A bird in the hand is
bad table manners.

L. L. Levinson

Watching the perpetual procession
of birds to and from the feeders is
one of the joys of the winter season.

Suzanne Mahler

The early bird usually wishes he'd
let someone else get up first.

Elliott Gould

As to the garden, it seems to
me its chief fruit is blackbirds.

William Morris

A bird in the hand is useless when you have to blow your nose.

Henny Youngman

Poor indeed is the garden in which birds find no homes.

Abram L. Urban

I once had a sparrow alight upon my shoulder for a moment, while I was hoeing in a village garden, and I felt that I was more distinguished by that circumstance that I should have been by any epaulet I could have worn.

Henry David Thoreau

Make sure your bird feeder is within easy reach of your cat – another way of ensuring that natural selection favours alert and hardy bird specimens.

Michael Powell, *The Accidental Gardener*

The early bird gets the
late one's breakfast.

Guy Pepper

It's hard to kill two birds
if one is stoned.

Brush Shiels

A RIPE OLD AGE

What do gardeners
do when they retire?

Bob Monkhouse

Live each day as if it were
your last, and garden as
though you will live forever.

Anonymous

❦

If I'm ever reborn, I want to
be a gardener – there's too
much to do for one lifetime!

Karl Foerster

❦

I want death to find me
planting my cabbages.

Michael de Montaigne

... though an old man, I am
but a young gardener.

Thomas Jefferson

———◦———

What exercise is more fitting, or
more appropriate of one who is
in the decline of life, than that of
superintending a well-ordered
garden? What more enlivens
the sinking mind? What is more
conducive to a long life?

Joseph Breck

———◦———

Old gardeners don't die. They
just throw in the trowel.

Audrey Austin

I know many elderly gardeners but
the majority are young at heart.

Allan Armitage

I'm not ageing, I just need re-potting.

Anonymous

WORKING OVER-THYME

Early to bed, early
to rise, work like
hell, fertilise.

Emily Whaley

What a man needs
in gardening is a
cast-iron back,
with a hinge in it.

Charles Dudley Warner

In order to live off a garden, you
practically have to live in it.

Frank McKinney Hubbard

Flowers are not made by
singing 'Oh, how beautiful,'
and sitting in the shade.

Rudyard Kipling

When you pray for
potatoes, grab a hoe.

Mrs Jamieson

All good work is done the way
ants do things: little by little.

Lafcadio Hearn

Any garden demands as much
of its maker as he has to give.

Elizabeth Lawrence

When your garden is finished I hope
it will be more beautiful than you
anticipated, require less care than
you expected, and have cost only a
little more than you had planned.

Thomas D. Church

The more help a man has in his garden, the less it belongs to him.

William M. Davies

And he gave it for his opinion that whoever could make two ears of corn, or two blades of grass, to grow upon a spot of ground where only one grew before, would deserve better of mankind, and do more essential service to his country, than the whole race of politicians put together.

Jonathan Swift, *Gulliver's Travels*

WEED 'EM AND REAP

Give weeds an
inch and they'll
take your yard.
Anonymous

What is a weed? A plant whose
virtues have not yet been discovered.

Ralph Waldo Emerson

...a plant that has mastered
every survival skill except for
learning how to grow in rows.

Doug Larson's definition of a weed

Sweet flowers are slow
and weeds make haste.

William Shakespeare

A garden is an awful responsibility.
You never know what you
may be aiding to grow in it.

Charles Dudley Warner

Weeds are nobody's guests:
more like squatters.

Norman Nicholson

But make no mistake: the weeds
will win: nature bats last.

Robert M. Pyle

A weed is no more than
a flower in disguise.

James Russell Lowell, *The Growth of a Legend*

We can in fact only define a weed, *mutatis mutandis*, in terms of the well-known definition of dirt – as matter out of place. What we call a weed is in fact merely a plant growing where we do not want it.

E. J. Salisbury, *The Living Garden*

I guess a good gardener always starts as a good weeder.

Amos Pettingill

A flower is an educated weed.

Luther Burbank

Plant and your spouse plants with you; weed and you weed alone.

Jean Jacques Rousseau

I've concluded weeds
must have brains.

Dianne Benson, *Dirt*

If you are a garden plant you are
regarded; well regarded, just as
long as you stay in the garden.

Davies Gilbert

A weed is a plant that is not only in
the wrong place, but intends to stay.

Sara Stein

If you water it and it dies, it's
a plant. If you pull it out and
it grows back, it's a weed.

Gerry Daly

A weed is but an unloved flower.

Ella Wilcox

Many things grow in the garden
that were never sown there.

Thomas Fuller

The philosopher who
said that work well
done never needs
doing over never
weeded a garden.

Ray D. Everson

A man of words
and not of deeds
Is like a garden
full of weeds.

Proverb

A BUTTERFLY
FLUTTERED BY

There is nothing
in a caterpillar that
tells you it's going
to be a butterfly.

R. Buckminster Fuller

What's a butterfly garden
without butterflies?

Roy Rogers

A caterpillar who seeks to
know himself would never
become a butterfly.

Andre Gide

The butterfly counts not months
but moments, and has time enough.

Rabindranath Tagore

A garden is as static as a painting
until a butterfly brings it to life.

Jo Brewer

In nature a repulsive caterpillar
turns into a lovely butterfly. But
with humans it is the other way
around: a lovely butterfly turns
into a repulsive caterpillar.

Anton Chekhov

'Just living is not enough,'
said the butterfly.
'One must have sunshine,
freedom, and a little flower.'

Hans Christian Andersen

Happiness is a
butterfly, which, when
pursued, is always just
beyond your grasp,
but which, if you will
sit down quietly, may
alight upon you.

Nathaniel Hawthorne

Have you enjoyed this book? If so, why not write a review on your favourite website?

Thanks very much for buying this Summersdale book.

www.summersdale.com